#4 TOMB OF THE FANGPYRE

GREG FARSHTEY • Writer
JOLYON YATES • Artist
JAYJAY JACKSON • Colourist
BRIAN SENKA • Letterer

TITAN
COMICS

D0293944

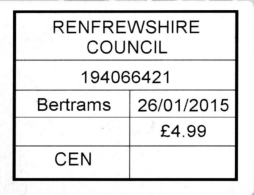

RENFREWSHIRE COUNCIL	
194066421	
Bertrams	26/01/2015
	£4.99
CEN	

LEGO® NINJAGO™ Masters of Spinjitzu
Volume 4: Tomb of the Fangpyre

Greg Farshtey – Writer
Jolyon Yates – Artist
JayJay Jackson – Colourist
Bryan Senka – Letterer

Published by Titan Comics, a division of Titan Publishing Group Ltd., 144 Southwark St., London, SE1 0UP. LEGO NINJAGO: VOLUME #4: TOMB OF THE FANGPYRE. LEGO, the LEGO logo and Ninjago are trademarks of the LEGO Group ©2014 The LEGO Group. All rights reserved. All characters, events and institutions depicted herein are fictional. Any similarity between any of the names, characters, persons, events and/or institutions in this publication to actual names, characters, and persons, whether living or dead and/or institutions are unintended and purely coincidental. License contact for Europe: Blue Ocean Entertainment AG, Germany.

A CIP catalogue record for this title is available from the British Library.

Printed in China.

First published in the USA and Canada in June 2013 by Papercutz.

10 9 8 7 6 5 4 3 2 1

ISBN: 9781782761952

www.titan-comics.com

www.LEGO.com

MEET THE MASTERS
OF SPINJITZU...

JAY

COLE

ZANE

KAI

And the Master of the
Masters of Spinjitzu...

SENSEI WU

BEWARE!
YOU ARE ABOUT TO ENTER THE WORLD OF NINJAGO . . .

BEWARE!
FOR SOON YOU WILL ENTER THE TOMB OF THE FANGPYRE!

THIS WAY TO SERPENTINE STONE

OH, YOU'VE GOT TO BE KIDDING...

THIS WAY SERPENT STO

IF SOMEONE WANTS ME GOING ONE WAY, I'M GOING THE *OTHER* WAY.

Later...

NO POINT SEARCHING IN THE DARK. I'LL MAKE A FIRE AND CAMP FOR THE NIGHT.

THERE WE GO, A NICE, BLAZING--

...*PIECE OF ICE.* HUH?

YIII!

A FROZEN FIRE AND RED-HOT SNOW? WHAT KIND OF A *CRAZY* PLACE IS THIS?

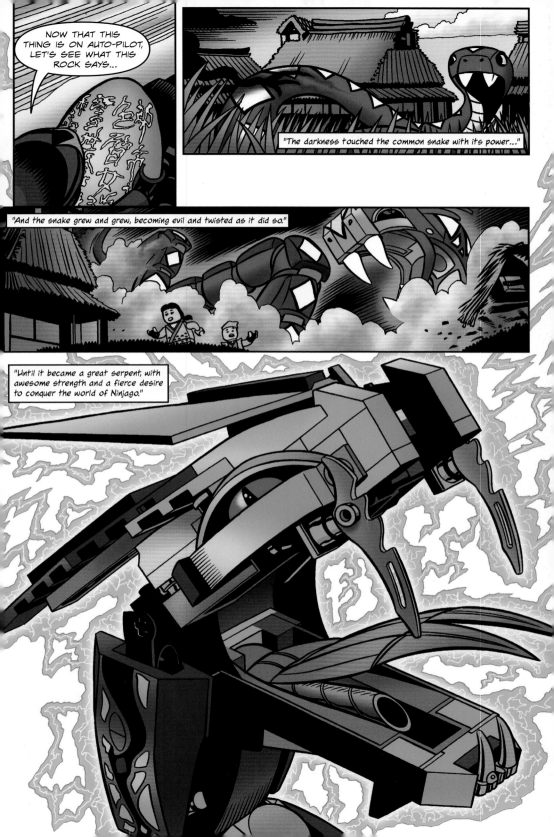

32

I *MUST* FIND A WAY TO DEFEAT THIS CREATURE, OR I WILL NEVER FIND MY STONE.

PERHAPS I CAN TRAP THE BEAST BETWEEN THOSE PILLARS LONG ENOUGH TO GET WHAT I CAME FOR, AND ESCAPE!

CRUNNNCHH

AT LAST! I FEARED I WOULD NEVER ESCAPE FROM THAT-- OH, *NO!*

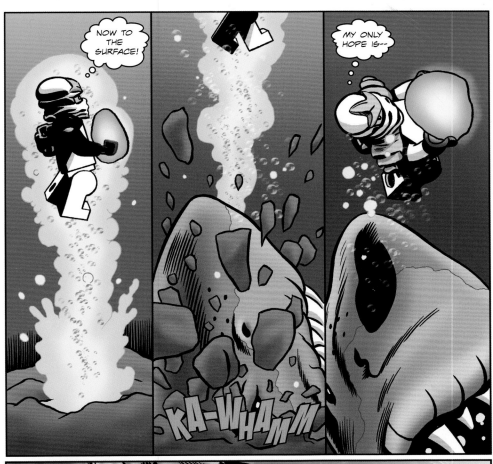

The power of the Golden Weapon of Spinjitzu causes a massive block of ice to form in the monster's jaws...

ITS POWERFUL JAWS WILL SHATTER THAT ICE IN AN INSTANT, BUT BY THAT TIME...

I WILL BE ON THE SURFACE...

...AND BACK ON DRY LAND. HERE'S HOPING MY FRIEND IS NOT AMPHIBIOUS.

NOW, WHAT TRUTHS DO YOU HAVE TO REVEAL, STONE?

"These four tribes of the Serpentine threatened to conquer Ninjago, and it seemed impossible to stop them."

"It took the creation of golden flutes to give the human inhabitants of this world the chance for victory."

"Using the flutes, the Serpentine were driven into tombs and sealed away... it was hoped, forever."

"But the Great Serpent was not defeated, merely delayed... and now it slumbers, waiting for the time when it will return again to menace Ninjago anew."

"And confident that none in this world know its secret."

In a daring move, Cole slams the tread assault into the wall...

CRASH

-:OOOF!:-

LLOYD GARMADON?! WHAT ARE YOU DOING HERE?

I'M HERE TO HELP YOU.

BY DROPPING A ROCK ON ME?

COME ON, LLOYD, WHY ARE YOU REALLY HERE?

THE FANGPYRE DON'T WANT YOU TO GET IT. ANYTHING THEY DON'T WANT, I DO WANT.

48

EXCELLENT! TWO DOWN, AND ONE TO GO-- FOOLISH FANGPYRE!

OH, NO!

AAAAAHHHH!

THE SNAKE WILL BE COMING BACK FOR ANOTHER PASS. SO MAYBE...

GET. ME. DOWN!

OWWWW!

WE'RE GOING FOR THE STONE, RIGHT NOW. WHERE IS IT?

I DON'T KNOW!

MAYBE THE SNAKES IN THOSE RATTLECOPTERS KNOW-- WANT TO GO BACK AND ASK?

OKAY, OKAY... MAYBE THEY SAID SOMETHING ABOUT UNDER THE ARCH.

LET'S GO, THEN, BEFORE THE FANGPYRE TRY SOMETHING ELSE.

53

None of them notice Cole unleashing his Spinjitzu power...

Not until it's *too late!*

GOT IT!

AND WE HAVE YOU!

TAKE THEM TO *THE TOMB!*

The Ninja's lucky streak seems to have come to an end, as Cole and Lloyd are marched off to the legendary tomb of the Fangpyre!

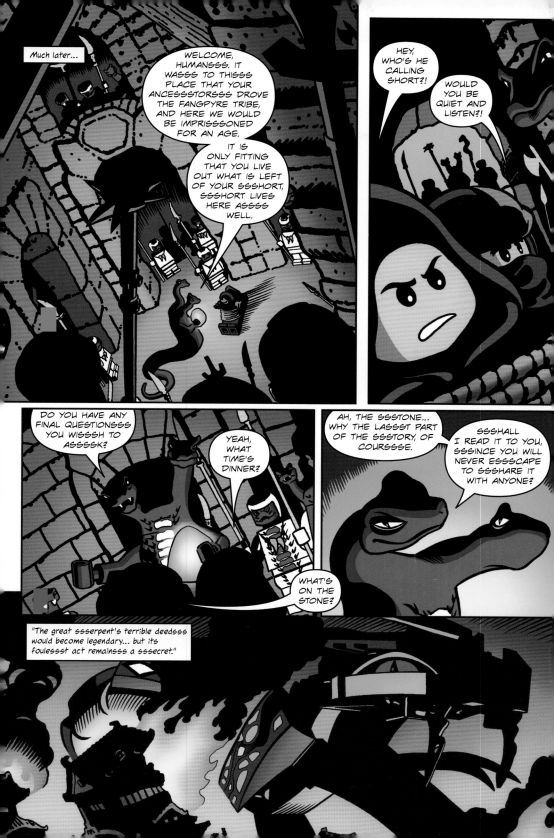

"When it wasss first touched by darknesss, the sssnake that would become the great sssserpent found its way into a garden."

"That brother wasss named Garmadon... and hisss terrible deedsss would become legendary too."

"The Garden wasss home to two brothers. The sssnake took one by sssurprise and bit him, and by doing that, it passssed its darknesss onto him."

DO YOU SSSEE THE ANSWER NOW, HUMANSSS? DO YOU UNDERSSSTAND THE POWER OF THE SSSECRET?

I DON'T GET IT. WHAT DOES ALL THIS HAVE TO DO WITH MY DAD?

I THINK I'M STARTING TO FIGURE IT OUT. CORRECT ME IF I'M WRONG, FANGTOM...

"Garmadon fought his brother, Sensei Wu, and lost, being banished to the Underworld," explains Cole...

"Later, he unleashed skeleton armies on Ninjago and tricked my team into helping him escape his exile. He hasn't been seen since."

GARMADON LOST EVERYTHING WHEN HE TURNED BAD-- HIS BROTHER, HIS FREEDOM, AND EVEN NOW, HE HAS NOTHING BUT A DESIRE FOR POWER AND REVENGE.

BUT IF NONE OF THIS WAS REALLY HIS FAULT...

WHAT THE GREAT SSSERPENT CAN DO, IT CAN UNDO.

IN RETURN FOR AN ALLIANCE AND HISSS AID IN OUR CONQUESSST OF THIS MUDBALL PLANET, THE SSSERPENTINE CAN GIVE HIM BACK HISSS HONOR, HISSS FAMILY, ALL THAT HE DOESSS NOT HAVE NOW.

SO DAD WOULD HAVE TO DO SOMETHING REALLY BAD TO BECOME GOOD AGAIN?

AND ONCE HE WAS GOOD, HE WOULD FEEL TERRIBLE ABOUT WHAT HE HAD DONE FOR THE REST OF HIS LIFE.

IT'S A LOUSY DEAL, AND SINCE HE'S NOT HERE, I'LL ANSWER FOR HIM--

Speaking of Lloyd's new friends, well, they are keeping busy...

LLOYD
GARMADON

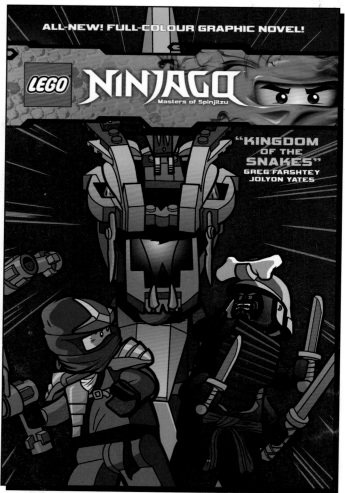